Pandora

Voltaire

Translation by William F. Fleming

©2011 Wilder Publications

Wilder Publications, Inc.
PO Box 10641
Blacksburg, VA 24063

ISBN 10: 1-61720-249-5
ISBN 13: 978-1-61720-249-0

First Edition

10 9 8 7 6 5 4 3 2 1

Contents

Dramatis Personæ

Prometheus, a Son of Heaven and Earth, A Demi-God.
Pandora.
Jupiter.
Mercury.
Nemesis.
Nymphs.
Titans.
Celestial Deities.
Infernal Deities.

ACT I.

The scene represents a fine country, with mountains at a distance.

SCENE I.

Prometheus, Chorus of Nymphs, Pandora.

[At the farther end of the stage, lying down in an alcove.]

Prometheus: In vain, Pandora, do I call on thee, My lovely work; alas! thou hearest me not, All stranger as thou art to thy own charms, And to Prometheus' love: the heart I formed Is still insensible; thy eyes are void Of motion; still the ruthless power of Jove Denies thee life, and drives me to despair: Whilst nature breathes around thee, and the birds In tender notes express their passion, thou Art still inanimate; death holds thee still Beneath his cruel empire.

SCENE II.

Prometheus, the Titans, Enceladus, Typhon, etc.

Enceladus and Typhon: Child of Earth And Heaven, thy cries have raised the forest; speak; Who amongst the gods hath wronged Prometheus?

Prometheus: [Pointing to Pandora.] Jove Is jealous of my work divine; he fears That altars will be raised to my Pandora; He cannot bear to see the earth adorned With such a peerless object; he denies To grant her life, and makes my woes eternal.

Typhon: That proud usurper Jove did ne'er create Our nobler souls; life, and its sacred flame, Come not from him.

Enceladus: [Pointing to his brother Typhon.] We are the sons of Night And Tartarus: To thee, eternal night, we pray, Thou wert long before the day; Let then to Janarus Olympus yield.

Typhon: Let the unrelenting Jove Join the jealous gods above; Life and all its blessings flow From hell, and from the gods below.

Prometheus and the Two Titans: Come from the centre, gods of night profound, And animate her beauty; let your power Assist our bold emprize!

Prometheus: Your voice is heard, The day looks pale, and the astonished earth Shakes from its deep foundations: Erebus Appears before us. [The scene changing represents chaos; all the gods of hell come upon the stage.]

Chorus of Infernal Deities: Light is hateful to our eyes, Jove and heaven we despise; The guilty race, as yet unborn, must go With us to hell's profoundest depths below.

Nemesis: The waves of Lethe, and the flames of hell, Shall ravage all: speak, whom must Janarus In its dark womb embrace?

Prometheus: I love the earth, And would not hurt it: to that beauteous object [Pointing to Pandora] Have I given birth; but Jove denies it power To breathe, to think, to love, and to be happy.

The Three Parcæ: All our glory, and our joy, Is to hurt, and to destroy; Heaven alone can give it breath, We can nought bestow but death.

Prometheus: Away then, ye destroyers, ye are not The deities Prometheus shall adore; Hence to your gloomy seats, ye hateful powers, And leave the world in peace.

Nemesis: Tremble thou, for thou shalt prove Soon the fatal power of love: We will unchain the fiends of war, And death's destructive gates unbar. [The infernal deities disappear, and the country resumes its verdure: the nymphs of the woods range themselves on each side of the stage.]

Prometheus: [To the Titans.] Why would ye call forth from their dark abyss The foes of nature, to obscure the light Of these fair regions? From hell Pandora never shall receive That flame divine which only heaven should give.

Enceladus: Since, good Prometheus, 'tis thy dear delight To scatter blessings o'er this new abode, Thou best deservest to be its master: haste To yon blest regions, and snatch thence the flame Celestial, form a soul, and be thyself The great Creator.

Prometheus: Love's in heaven; he reigns O'er all the gods: I'll throw his darts around, And light up his fierce fires: he is my god, And will assist Prometheus.

Chorus of Nymphs: Fly to the immortal realms above, And penetrate the throne of Jove; The world to thee shall altars raise, And millions celebrate thy praise.

ACT II.

The scene represents the same country; Pandora inanimate reclining in the alcove; a flaming chariot descends from heaven.

Prometheus, Pandora, Nymphs, Titans, etc.

A Dryad: Ye woodland nymphs, rise from your fair abode, And sing the praises of the demi-god; Who returns from above In the chariot of love?

Chorus of Nymphs: Ye verdant lawns, and opening flowers, Ye springs which lavish nature's powers; Ye hills that bear the impending sky, Put on your fairest forms to meet his eye.

Prometheus: [Descending from the chariot, with a torch in his hand.] Ravished from heaven I bring to happier earth Love's sacred flame, more brilliant than the light Of glittering day, and to Jove's boasted thunder Superior.

Chorus of Nymphs: Go, thou enlivening, animating soul, Through nature's every work, pervade the whole; To earth, to water, and to air impart, Thy vivid power, and breathe o'er every heart.

Prometheus: [Coming near to Pandora.] And may this precious flame inspire thy frame With life and motion! earth, assist my purpose! Rise, beauteous object, love commands thee; haste, Obey his voice; arise, and bless Prometheus! [Pandora rises, and comes forward.]

Chorus: She breathes, she lives; O love, how great thy power!

Pandora: Whence, and what am I? to what gracious powers Owe I my life and being? [A symphony is heard at a distance.] Hark! my ears Are ravished with enchanting sounds; my eyes With beauteous objects filled on every side: What wonders hath my kind creator spread Around me! O where is he? I have thought And reason to enlighten me: O earth, Thou art not my mother; some benignant god Produced me: yes, I feel him in my heart. [She sits down by the side of a fountain.] What do I see! myself, in this fair fountain, That doth reflect the face of heaven? the more I see this image, sure the more I ought To thank the gods who made me.

Nymphs and Titans: [Dancing round her.] Fair Pandora, Daughter of heaven, let thy charms inspire An equal flame, and fan the mutual fire.

Pandora: What lovely object that way draws my eyes? [To Prometheus.] Of all I see in these delightful mansions, Nought pleases like thyself; 'twas thou alone Who gavest me life, and I will live for thee.

Prometheus: Before those lovely eyes could see Their author, they enchanted me; Before that tongue could speak, Prometheus loved thee.

Pandora: Thou lovest me then, dear author of my life, And my heart owns its master; for to thee It flies with transport: have I said too much, Or not enough?

Prometheus: O thou canst never say Too much; thou speakest the language of pure love And nature: thus may lovers always speak!

Duet: God of my heart, eternal power, Great love, enliven every hour; Thy reign begins, and may thy transports prove The reign of pleasure is the reign of love!

Prometheus: But hark! the thunder rolls; thick clouds of darkness, As envious of the earth's new happiness, Disturb our joys: what horrors throng around me! Hark! the earth shakes, and angry lightnings pierce The vault of heaven: what power thus moves the world From its foundations? [A car descends, on which are seated Mercury, Discord, Nemesis, etc.]

Mercury: Some rash hand hath stolen The sacred fire from heaven: to expiate The dire offence, Pandora, thou must go Before the high tribunal of the gods.

Prometheus: O cruel tyrant!

Pandora: Dread commands!

Mercury: Obey: Thou must to heaven.

Pandora: I was in heaven already, When I beheld the object of my love.

Prometheus: Have pity, cruel gods!

Prometheus and Pandora, Barbarians, stay.

Mercury: Haste, offenders, haste away, Jove commands, you must obey: Bear her, ye winds, to heaven's eternal mansions. [The car mounts and disappears.]

Prometheus: The cruel tyrants, jealous of my bliss, Have torn her from me; she was the lovely work Of my own hands: I have done more than Jove Could ever do: Pandora's charming eyes, Soon as they opened, told me that she loved: Thou jealous god! but thou shalt feel my wrath, And I will brave thy power: for know, usurper, Less dreadful far will all thy thunders prove, Than bold Prometheus fired by hopeless love.

ACT III.

The scene represents the palace of Jupiter.

Jupiter, Mercury.

Jupiter: O Mercury, I've seen this lovely object, Earth's fair production; heaven is in her eye, The graces dwell around her, and my heart Is sacrificed a victim to her charms.

Mercury: And she shall answer to thy love.

Jupiter: O no: Terror is mine, and power; I reign supreme O'er earth, and hell, and heaven; but love alone Can govern hearts: malicious, cruel fate, When it divided this fair universe, Bestowed the better part on mighty love.

Mercury: What fearest thou? fair Pandora scarce hath seen The light of day; and thinkest thou that she loves?

Jupiter: Love is a passion learned with ease; and what Cannot Pandora do? she is a woman, And handsome: but I will retire a moment, Enchant her eyes, and captivate her heart: Ye heavens! in vain, alas! ye shine, for nought Have you so fair, so beauteous as Pandora. [He retires.]

Pandora: Scarce have these eyes beheld the light of day, Scarce have they looked on him I loved, when lo! 'Tis all snatched from me; death, they say, will come And take me soon: O I have felt him sure Already: is not death the sudden loss Of those we love? O give me back, ye gods, To earth, to that delightful grove where first I saw my kind creator, when at once I breathed and loved: O envied happiness! [The gods, with their several attributes, come upon the stage.]

Chorus of Gods: Let heaven rejoice At the glad voice Of heaven's eternal king.

Neptune: Let the sea's bosom—

Pluto: And the depths of hell—

Chorus of Gods: To distant worlds his endless praises tell. Let heaven rejoice, etc.

Pandora: How all conspires to threaten and alarm me! O how I hate and fear this dazzling splendor! Another's merit how can I approve, Or bear the praise of aught but him I love?

The Three Graces: Love's fair daughter, here remain, Thou in right of him shalt reign; Heaven thy chosen seat shall be, Earth in vain shall wish for thee.

Pandora: All affrights me, Nought delights me, Alas! a desert had more charms for me. Hence, ye idle visions; cease, Discordant sounds, [A Symphony is heard.] And give me peace. [Jupiter comes forth out of a cloud.]

Jupiter: Thou art the best and fairest charm of nature, Well worthy of eternity: from earth Sprang thy weak body; but thy purer soul Partakes of heaven's unalterable fire, And thou wert born for gods alone: with Jove Taste then the sweets of immortality.

Pandora: I scorn thy gift, and rather would be nothing, From whence I sprang; thy immortality, Without the lovely object I adore, Is but eternal punishment.

Jupiter: Fair creature, Thou knowest not I am master of the thunder: Canst thou in heaven look back to earth?

Pandora: That earth Is my abode; there first I learned to love.

Jupiter: 'Twas but the shadow of it, in a world Unworthy of that noble flame, which here Alone can burn unquenchable.

Pandora: Great Jove, Content with glory and with splendor, leave To earthly lovers happiness and joy: Thou art a god; O hear my humble prayer! A gracious god should make his creatures happy.

Jupiter: Thou shalt be happy, and in thee I hope For bliss supreme: ye powerful pleasures, you Who dwell around me, now exert your charms, Deceive her lovely eyes, and win her heart. [The Pleasures dance around her and sing.]

Chorus of Pleasures: Thou with us shalt reign and love, Thou alone art worthy Jove.

A Single Voice: Nought has earth but shadows vain, Of pleasures followed close by pain; Soon her winged transports fly, Soon her roses fade and die.

Chorus: Thou with us shalt reign and love, Thou alone art worthy Jove.

Single Voice: Here the brisk and sportive hours Shall cull thee ever-blooming flowers; Time has no wings, he cannot fly, And love is joined to immortality.

Chorus: Thou with us shalt reign and love, Thou alone art worthy Jove.

Pandora: Ye tender pleasures, ye increase my flame, And ye increase my pain: if happiness Is yours to give, O bear it to my love.

Jupiter: Is this the sad effect of all my care, To make a rival happy? [Enter Mercury.]

Mercury: Assume thy lightnings, Jove, and blast thy foe; Prometheus is in arms, the Titans rage, And threaten heaven; mountain on mountain piled, They scale the skies; already they approach.

Jupiter: Jove has the power to punish; let them come.

Pandora: And wilt thou punish? thou, who art the cause Of all his miseries; thou art a jealous tyrant: Go on, and love me; I shall hate thee more; Be that thy punishment.

Jupiter: I must away: Rive them, ye thunder-bolts.

Pandora: Have mercy, Jove!

Jupiter: [To Mercury.] Conduct Pandora to a place of safety: The happy world was wrapped in peace profound, A beauty comes, and nought is seen but ruin. [He goes out.]

Pandora: [Alone] O fatal charms! would I had ne'er been born! Beauty and love, and every gift divine, But make me wretched: if, all-powerful Love, Thou didst create me, now relieve my sorrows; Dry up my tears, bid war and slaughter cease, And give to heaven and earth eternal peace.

ACT IV.

The scene represents the Titans armed, mountains at a distance, with giants throwing them on each other.

Enceladus: Fear not, Prometheus, nature feels thy wrongs, And joins with us in just revenge: behold These pointed rocks, and shaggy mountains; soon The jealous tyrants all shall sink beneath them.

Prometheus: Now, earth, defend thyself, and combat heaven: Trumpets and drums, now shall ye first be heard: March, Titans, follow me: the seat of gods Is your reward; be fair Pandora mine. [They march to the sound of trumpets.]

Chorus of Titans: Arm, ye valiant Titans, arm, Spread around the dread alarm: Let proud immortals tremble on their thrones.

Prometheus: Their thunder answers to our trumpets' voice. [Thunder is heard; a car descends, bearing the gods towards the mountains: Pandora is seated near Jupiter; Prometheus speaks.] Jove gives the dreadful signal; haste, begin The battle. [The giants rise towards heaven.]

Chorus of Nymphs: Earth, and hell, and heaven confounded, All with terrors are surrounded: Cease, ye gods, and Titans, cease Your cruel wars, and give us peace.

Titans: Yield, cruel tyrants.

Gods: Rebels, fly.

Titans: Yield, heaven, to earth.

Gods: Die, rebels, die.

Pandora: O heaven! O earth! ye Titans, and ye gods, O cease your rage, all perish for Pandora: I have made the world unhappy.

Titans: Draw Your arrows now.

Gods: Strike, thunders.

Titans: Hurl down heaven.

Gods: Destroy the earth.

Both: Yield, cruel tyrants—rebels fly— Yield, earth, to heaven—die, rebels, die. [A dead silence for a time; a bright cloud descends; Destiny appears, seated in the middle of it.]

Destiny: Cease, hostile powers, attend to me, And hear the will of Destiny. [Silence ensues.]

Prometheus: Unalterable being, power supreme, Speak thy irrevocable doom; attend, Ye tyrants, and obey.

Chorus: Speak, the gods must yield to thee; Speak, immortal Destiny.

Destiny: [In the middle of the gods, who throng round him.] Hear me, ye gods; another world this day Brings forth: meantime let every gift adorn Pandora; and you, Titans, who 'gainst heaven Have raised rebellious war, receive your doom, Beneath these mountains sunk forever groan. [The rocks fall upon them; the chariot of the gods descends to earth; Pandora is restored to Prometheus.]

Jupiter: O fate, my empire yields to thee, Jove submits to destiny: Thou art obeyed; but from this hour let earth And heaven be disunited: Nemesis, Come forth. [Nemesis advances from the bottom of the stage, and Jupiter proceeds.] Nemesis, thy aid impart, Pierce the cruel beauty's heart; My vengeance let Pandora know, In the gifts that I bestow: Let heaven and earth henceforth be disunited.

ACT V.

The scene represents a grove, with the ruins of rocks scattered about it.

Prometheus, Pandora.

Pandora: [Holding a box in her hand.] And wilt thou leave me then? art thou subdued, Or art thou conqueror?

Prometheus: Victory is mine: If yet thou lovest me, love and destiny Speak for Prometheus.

Pandora: Wilt thou leave me then?

Prometheus: The Titans are subdued: lament their fate: I must assist them; let us teach mankind To succor the unhappy.

Pandora: Stay a moment: Behold thy victory: let us open this, It was the gift of Jove.

Prometheus: What wouldst thou do? A rival's gift is dangerous; 'tis some snare The gods have laid.

Pandora: Thou canst not think it.

Prometheus: Hear What I request of thee, and stay at least Till I return.

Pandora: Thou biddest, and I obey: I swear by love still to believe Prometheus.

Prometheus: Wilt thou then promise?

Pandora: By thyself I swear: All are obedient where they love.

Prometheus: Enough: I'm satisfied: and now, ye woodland nymphs, Begin your songs; sing earth restored to bliss; Let all be gay, for all was made for her.

First Nymph: Come, fair Pandora, come and prove An age of gold, of innocence, and love; And, like thy parent Nature, be immortal.

Second Nymph: No longer now shall earth affrighted mourn, By cruel war her tender bosom torn: Pleasures now on pleasures flow, Happiness succeeds to woe: The flowers their fragrant odors yield; Who would wither the fair field? The blest creation teems with mirth and joy, And nature's work what tyrant would destroy?

The Chorus: [Repeats.] Come, fair Pandora, come and prove An age of gold, etc.

First Nymph: See! to Pandora Mercury appears, And ratifies great Nature's kind decree. [The nymphs retire: Pandora advances with Nemesis, under the figure of Mercury.]

Nemesis: Already I have told thee, base Prometheus Is jealous of thee, and exerts his power Like a harsh tyrant.

Pandora: O he is my lord, My king, my god, my lover, and my husband.

Nemesis: Why then forbid thee to behold the gift Of generous heaven?

Pandora: His fearful love's alarmed, And I would wish to have no will but his.

Nemesis: He asks too much, Pandora, nor hath done What thou deservest: he might have given thee beauties Which now thou hast not.

Pandora: He hath formed my heart Tender and kind; he charms and he adores me; What could he more?

Nemesis: Thy charms will perish.

Pandora: Ha! Thou makest me tremble.

Nemesis: This mysterious box Will make thy charms immortal; thou wilt be Forever beauteous, and forever happy: Thy husband shall be subject to thy power, And thou shalt reign unrivalled in his love.

Pandora: He is my only lord, and I would wish To be immortal, but for my Prometheus.

Nemesis: Fain would I open thy fair eyes, and bless thee With every good; would make thee please forever.

Pandora: But dost thou not abuse my innocence? And canst thou be so cruel?

Nemesis: Who would hurt Such beauty?

Pandora: I should die with grief, if e'er I disobliged the sovereign of my heart.

Nemesis: O in the name of Nature, in the name Of thy dear husband, listen to my voice!

Pandora: That name has conquered, and I will believe thee. [She opens the box; darkness is spread over the stage, and a voice heard from below.] Ha! what thick cloud thus o'er my senses spreads Its fatal darkness? thou deceitful god! O I am guilty, and I suffer for it.

Nemesis: I must away: Jove is revenged, and now I will return to hell. [Nemesis vanishes: Pandora faints away on the grass.]

Prometheus: [Advancing from the farther end of the stage.] O fatal absence! dreadful change! what star Of evil influence thus deforms the face Of Nature? where's my dear Pandora? why Answers she not to my complaining voice? O my Pandora! but behold, from hell Let loose, the monsters rise, and rush upon us. [Furies and demons running on the stage.]

Furies: The time is come when we shall reign: Fear and grief, remorse and pain, From this great decisive hour, O'er the world shall spread their power; Death shall come, a bitter draught, By the Furies hither brought.

Prometheus: That cruel guest shall powers infernal bring? And must the earth lose her eternal spring? To time, and dire disease, and horrid vice, Shall mortals fall a helpless sacrifice? The nymphs lament our fate: Pandora, hear And answer to my griefs! she comes, but seems Insensible.

Pandora: I am not worthy of thee: I have destroyed mankind, deceived my husband, And am alone the guilty cause of all: Strike: I deserve it.

Prometheus: Can I punish thee?

Pandora: Strike, and deprive me of that wretched life Thou didst bestow.

Chorus of Nymphs: Tenderest lover, dry her tears, She is full of lover's fears; She is woman, therefore frail, Let her beauty then prevail.

Prometheus: Hast thou then, spite of all thy solemn vows, Opened the fatal box?

Pandora: Some cruel god Betrayed me: fatal curiosity! The work was thine: O every evil sprung From that accursed gift: undone Pandora!

Love: [Descending from heaven.] Love still remains, and every good is thine: [Scene changes, and represents the palace of love.] [Love proceeds.] For thee will I resist the power of fate; I gave to mortals being, and they ne'er Shall be unhappy whilst they worship me.

Pandora: Soul of my soul, thou comforter divine, O punish Jove; inspire his vengeful heart With double passion for the blessed Pandora.

Prometheus and Pandora: Heaven shall pierce our hearts in vain With every grief, and every pain; With thee no pains torment, no pleasures cloy; With thee to suffer is but to enjoy.

love: Lovely hope, on mortals wait; Come, and gild their wretched state; All thy flattering joys impart. Haste, and live in every heart; Howe'er deceitful thou mayest be, Thou canst grant felicity, And make them happy in futurity.

Pandora: Fate would make us wretched here, But hope shall dry up every tear; In sorrow he shall give us rest, And make us even in anguish blest: Love shall preserve us from the paths of vice, And strew his flowers around the precipice.

End